LIL' MONSTER BIBS

I0893599

HAND-STITCHED GIFTS ANY BABY WOULD LOVE?

Yes! These Cross Stitch designs of zany little monsters will catch Baby's eye with their bright colors and whimsical features. By stitching them on purchased toddler or infant bibs with 14-count inserts, you can easily create cherished keepsakes while making mealtimes more fun for the little one. The sweet themes include "I Love You," "Hey Baby," and "Monster Play Time." They're excellent for shower gifts!

ABOUT JUDITH MCCABE

"Lil' Monster Bibs was inspired by what I hear from today's young mothers," says Judith McCabe. "They want to avoid the typical cross stitch bears and rubber duckies for their children. So I looked at non-traditional themes and contemporary colors for inspiration."

Judith has been interested in needlework since she learned to embroider in Girl Scouts. "Our troop made stuffed toys. Mine was a blue camel with black blanket stitch. I remember the pride I felt when it was added to the Toys for Tots box to be delivered to the Marines."

In the years since then, Judith has earned degrees in elementary education and fiber and mixed media. She enjoys teaching children the skills they need to express their visions. At one time, she owned a store that focused on children's parties and craft classes.

Lil' Monster Bibs is a reflection of Judith's own playful, creative nature. It is her first publication with Leisure Arts.

"Creating cross stitch is immensely satisfying," she says. "Whenever I travel, I take a notebook and color pencils with me—you never know where you might find the next idea for an exciting project!"

LEISURE ARTS, INC.
Maumelle, Arkansas

HeyBaby!

Along Came A Spider

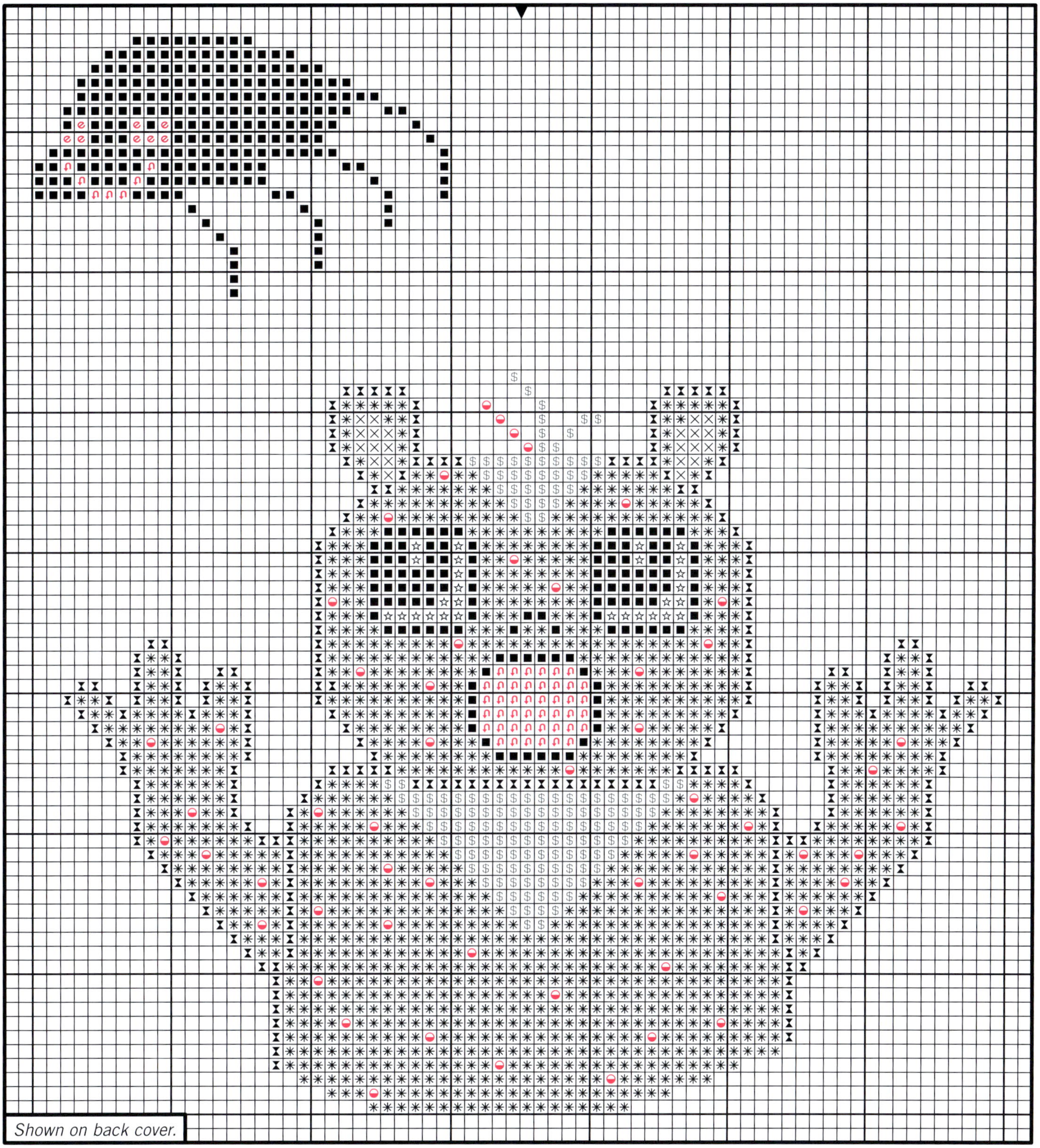

Shown on back cover.

Along Came A Spider (70w x 77h)

X	DMC	ANC.	COLOR
☆	blanc	2	white
■	310	403	black
⧗	807	168	teal
◒	900	333	dk orange
e	907	255	green
$	971	316	orange
✳	3766	167	aqua
∩	3804	63	dk pink
☒	3806	62	pink

Design was stitched on a 14 count Aida pink polka dot Charles Craft Baby Soft Infant Bib (design size 5" x 5½"), placing the design right above the binding and filling in stitching as necessary. Three strands of floss were used for Cross Stitch.

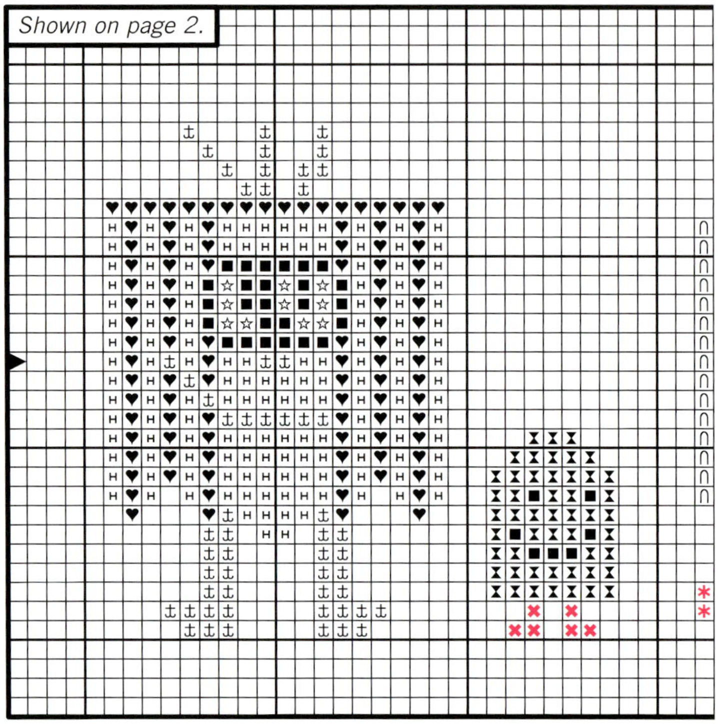

Shown on page 2.

Monster Play Time

Monster Play Time (106w x 31h)

X	DMC	ANC.	COLOR
☆	blanc	2	white
Λ	164	240	lt green
✖	209	109	lavender
✦	307	289	yellow
■	310	403	black
♡	666	46	red
Z	741	304	orange
6	913	204	green
❖	995	410	vy bright blue
8	996	433	bright blue
✳	3766	167	aqua

Design was stitched on a printed Charles Craft Velour Pullover Toddler Bib with a 14 count Aida insert (design size 7 5/8" x 2 1/4"). Three strands of floss were used for Cross Stitch.

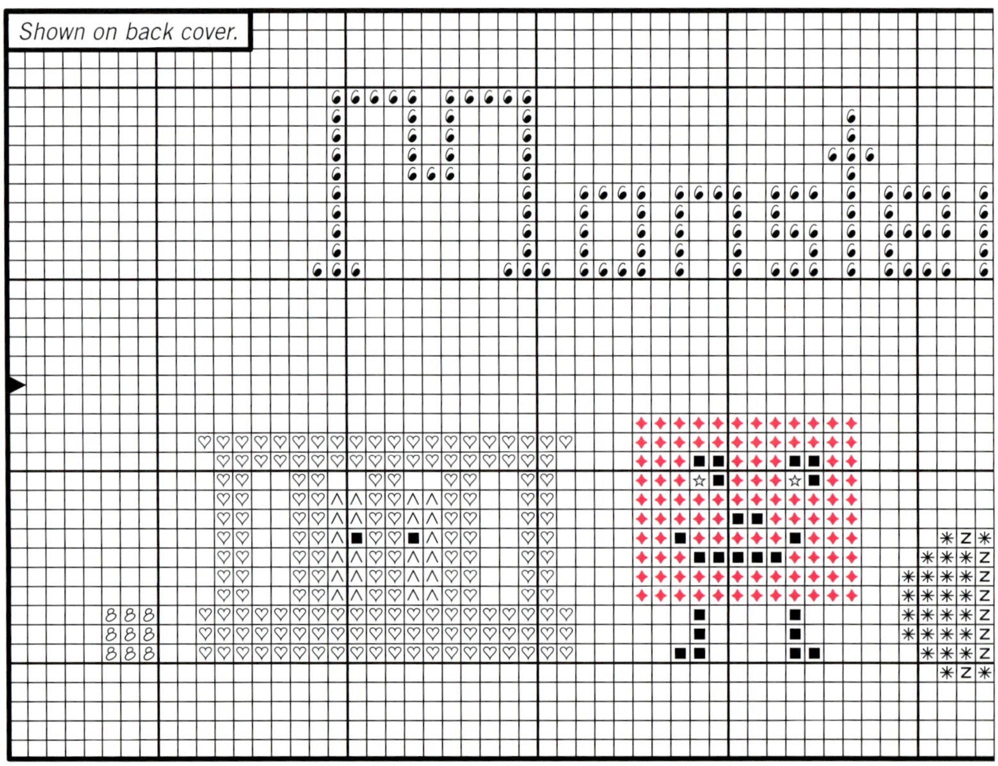

Shown on back cover.

Monster Group

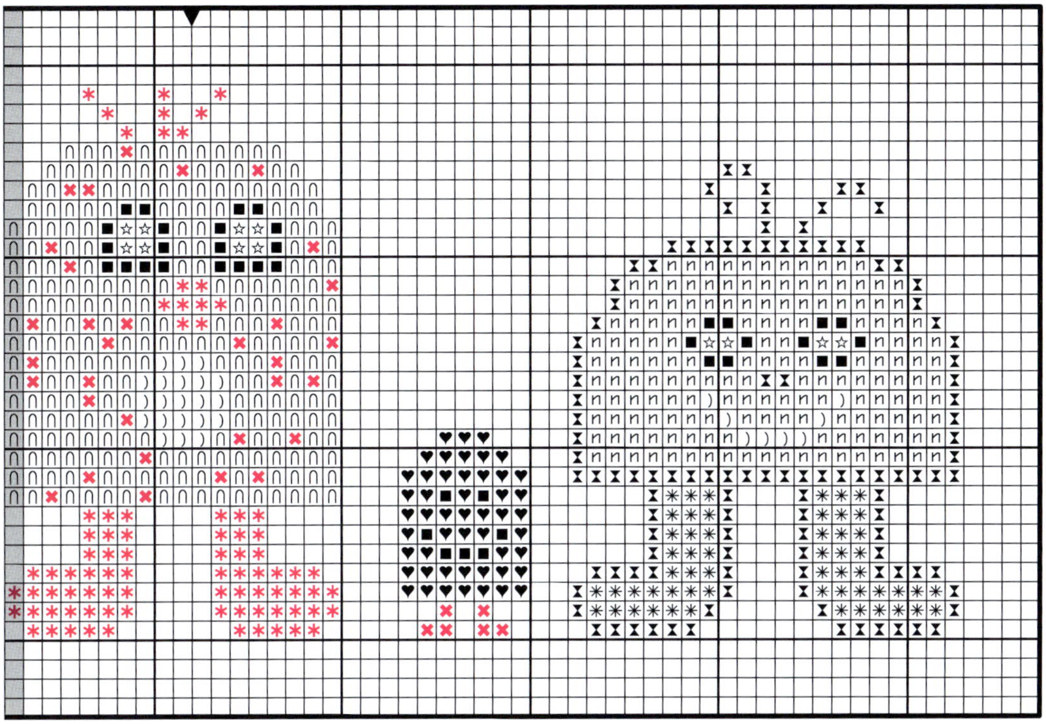

Monster Group (82w x 29h)

X	DMC	ANC.	COLOR
☆	blanc	2	white
■	310	403	black
♥	444	290	dk yellow
H	445	288	yellow
±	606	334	red orange
⧗	807	168	teal
n	955	206	mint
)	957	50	pink
✱	3347	266	olive
∩	3348	264	lt olive
✳	3766	167	lt teal
✖	3837	100	purple

Design was stitched on a white Charles Craft Velour Pullover Toddler Bib with a 14 count Aida insert (design size $5^{7}/_{8}$" x $2^{1}/_{8}$"). Three strands of floss were used for Cross Stitch.

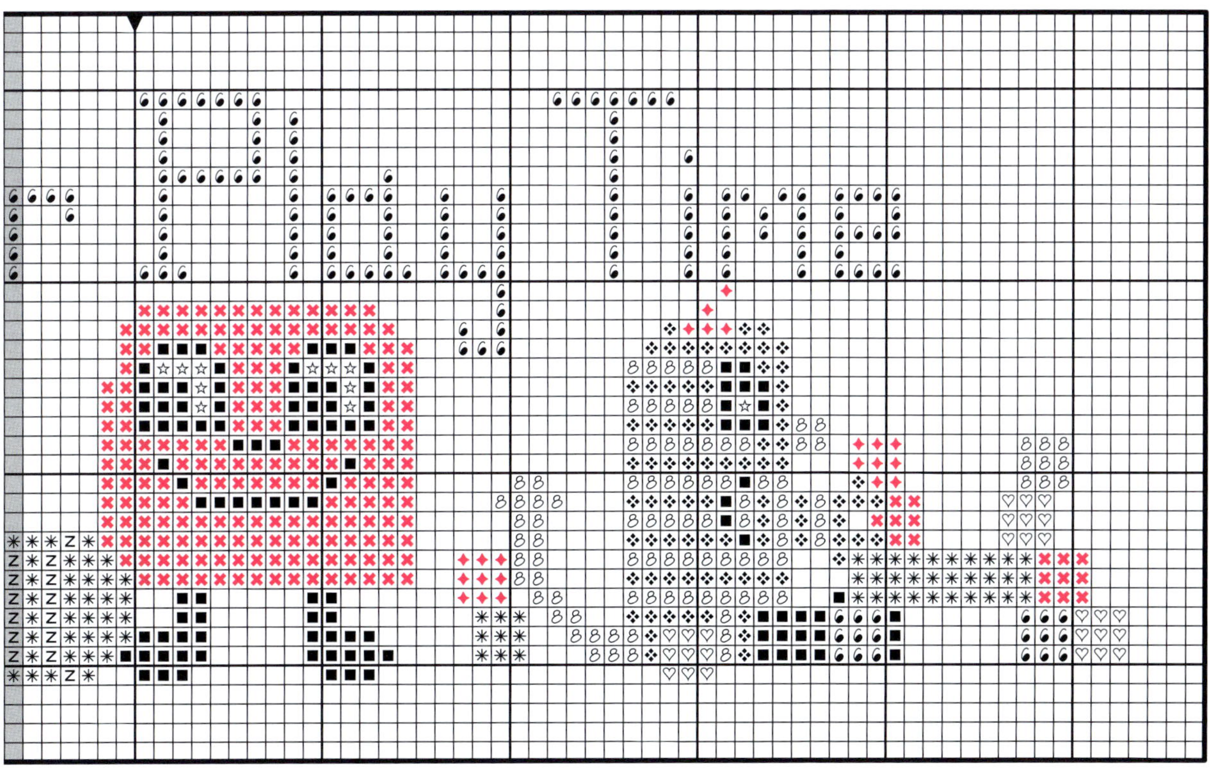

Peek-A-Boo

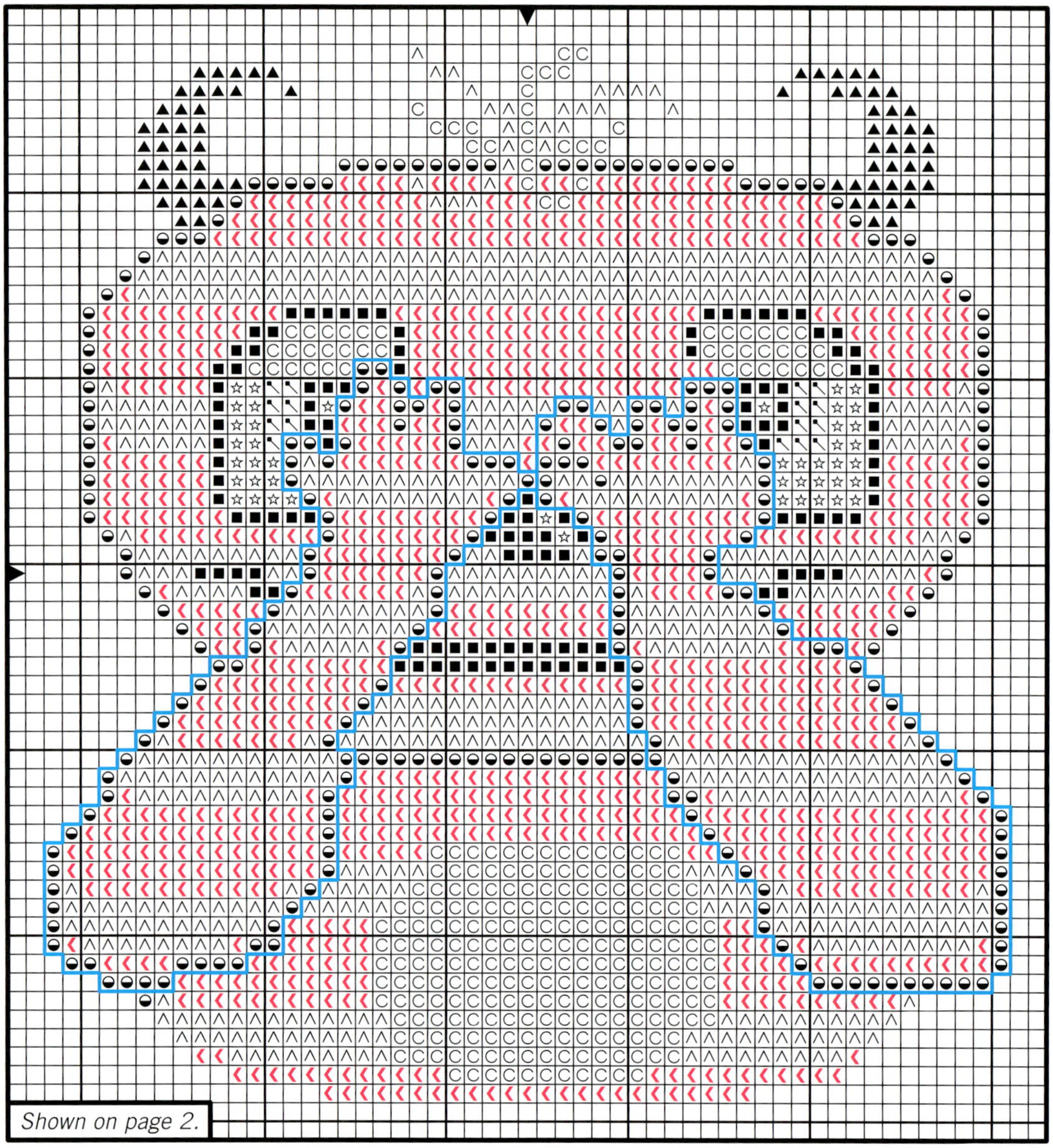

Shown on page 2.

Peek-A-Boo (53w x 57h)

X	DMC	ANC.	COLOR
☆	blanc	2	white
C	157	120	lt blue
∧	164	240	lt green
■	310	403	black

X	DMC	B'ST	ANC.	COLOR
◒	792	/	941	dk blue
❮	793		176	blue
▲	973		297	yellow
◥	988		243	green

Design was stitched on a 14 count Aida blue polka dot Charles Craft Baby Soft Infant Bib (design size 3⁷/₈" x 4¹/₈"). Three strands of floss were used for Cross Stitch and 1 strand for Backstitch.

Green Monster

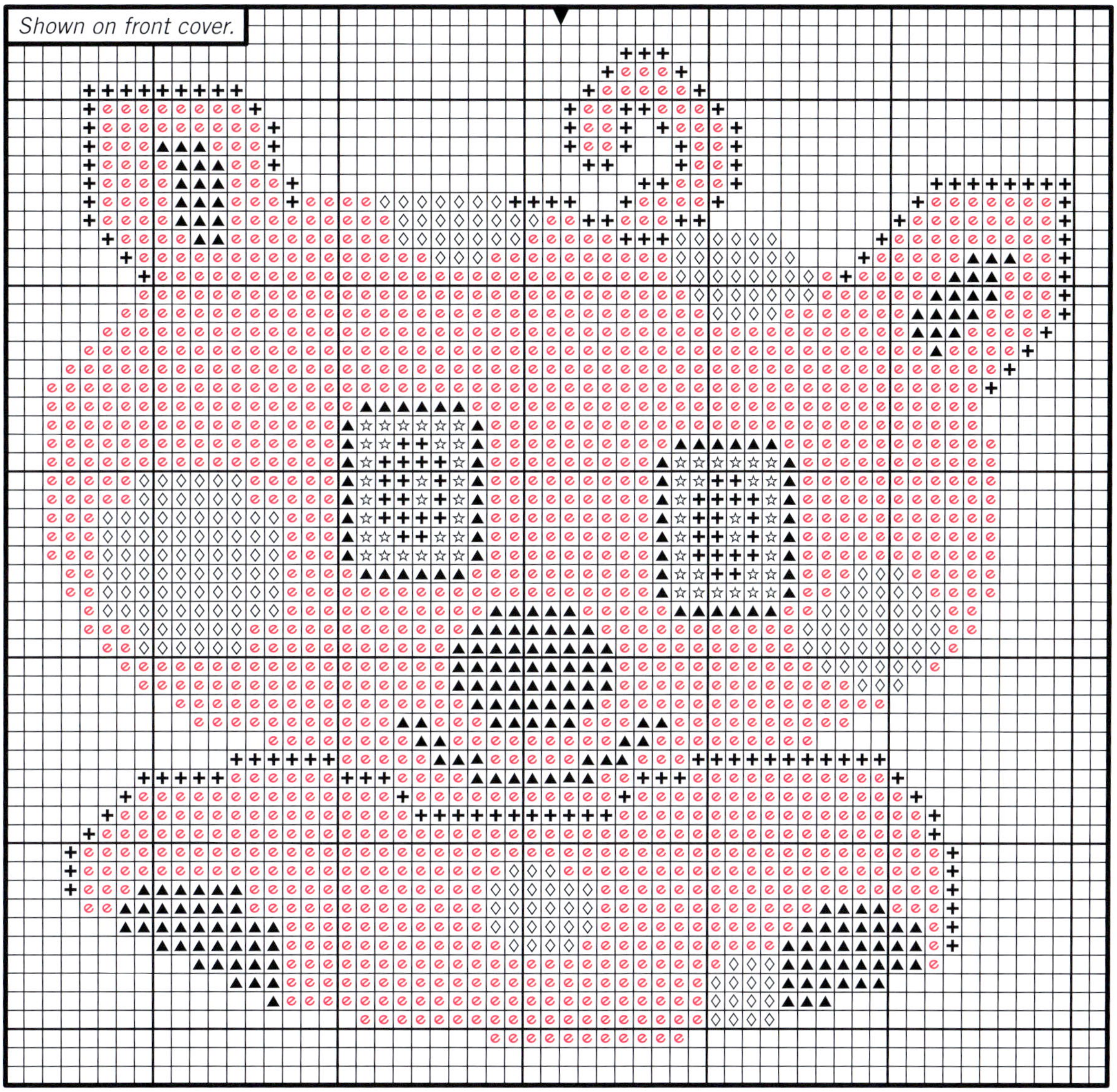

Green Monster (56w x 54h)

X	DMC	ANC.	COLOR
☆	blanc	2	white
▲	720	326	dk orange
◇	722	323	lt orange
e	906	256	green
+	907	255	dk green

Design was stitched on a 14 count Aida white Charles Craft Baby Soft Infant Bib (design size 4" x 3⁷/₈"), placing the design right above the binding and filling in stitching as necessary. Three strands of floss were used for Cross Stitch.

Shown on front cover.

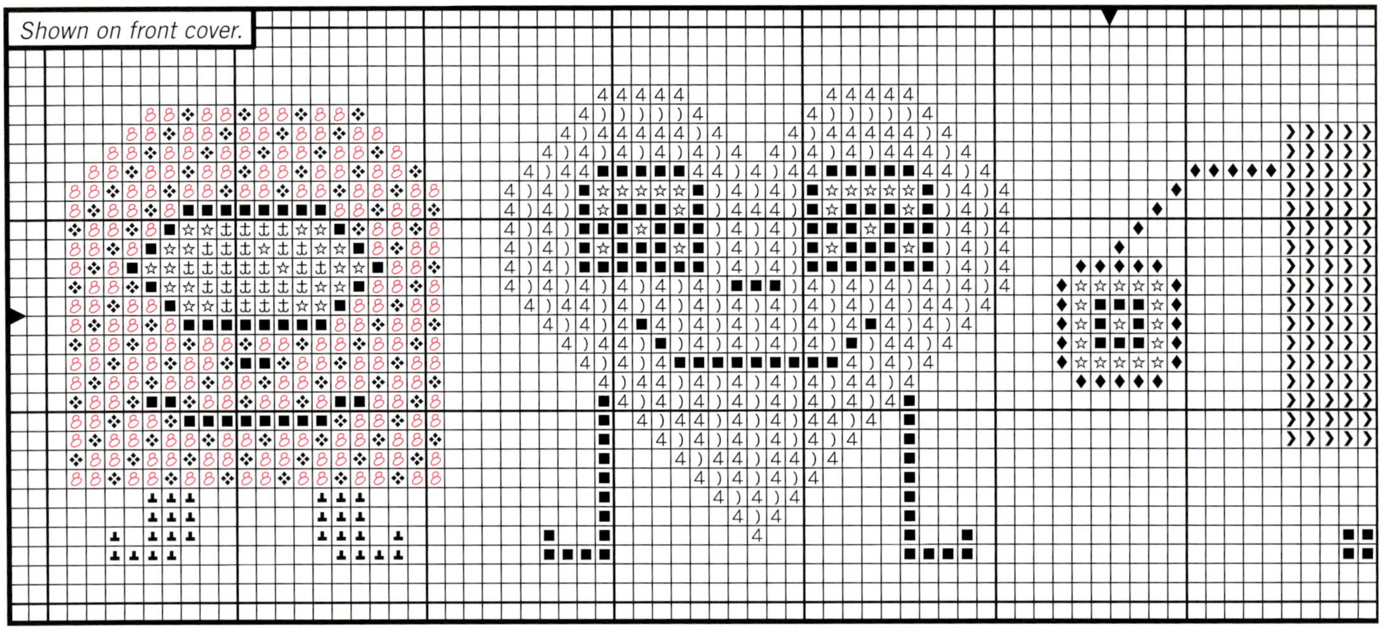

Hey Baby! (98w x 31h)

X	DMC	ANC.	COLOR
☆	blanc	2	white
✖	209	109	lavender
■	310	403	black
⚓	606	334	red orange
❯	703	238	green
4	956	40	pink
8	996	433	bright blue
★	3843	1089	turquoise

Design was stitched on a printed Charles Craft Velour Pullover Toddler Bib with a 14 count Aida insert (design size 7" x 2 1/4"). Three strands of floss were used for Cross Stitch.

Hey Baby!

Shown on page 2.

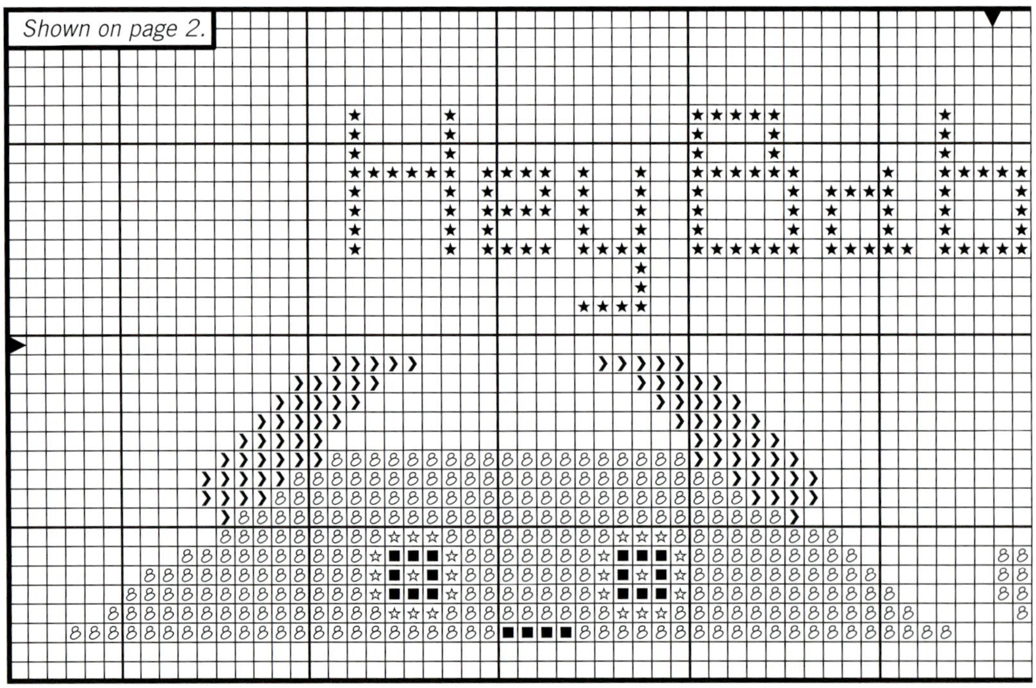

I ♥ U!

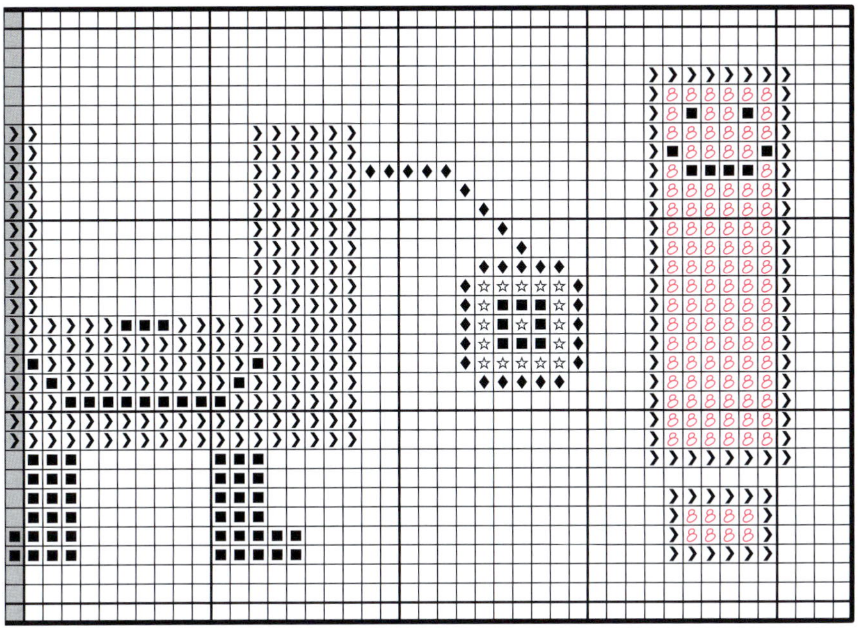

I♥U! (110w x 26h)

X	DMC	ANC.	COLOR
☆	blanc	2	white
◆	208	110	lavender
■	310	403	black
⚓	606	334	red orange
❯	703	238	green
⊥	797	132	dk blue
4	956	40	pink
)	957	50	lt pink
	995	410	vy bright blue
8	996	433	bright blue

Design was stitched on a pink Charles Craft Velour Pullover Toddler Bib with a 14 count Aida insert (design size 7⁷/₈" x 1⁷/₈"). Three strands of floss were used for Cross Stitch.

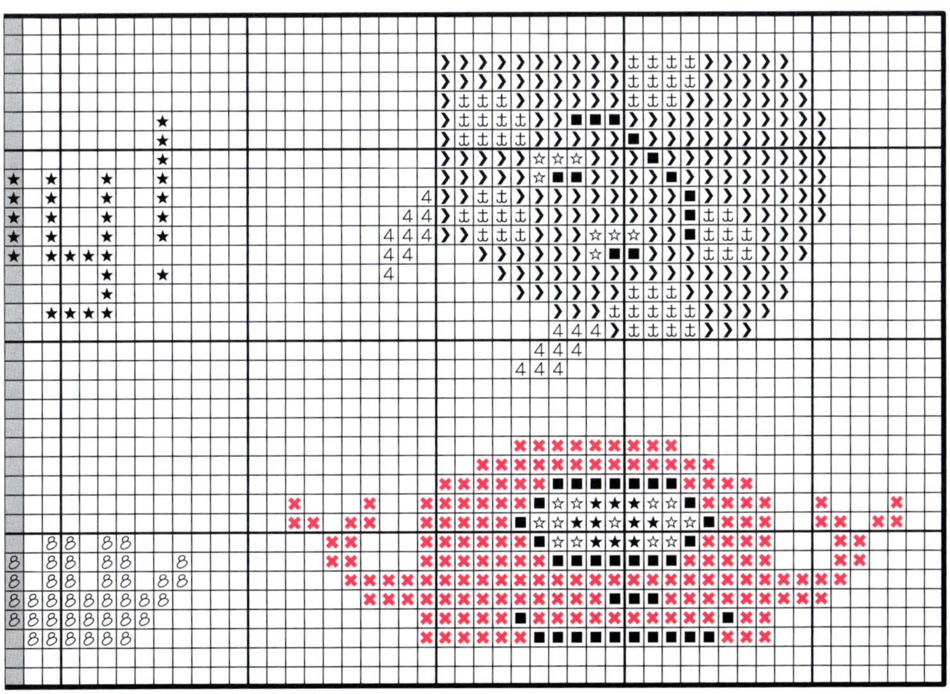

Polka Dotted Monster

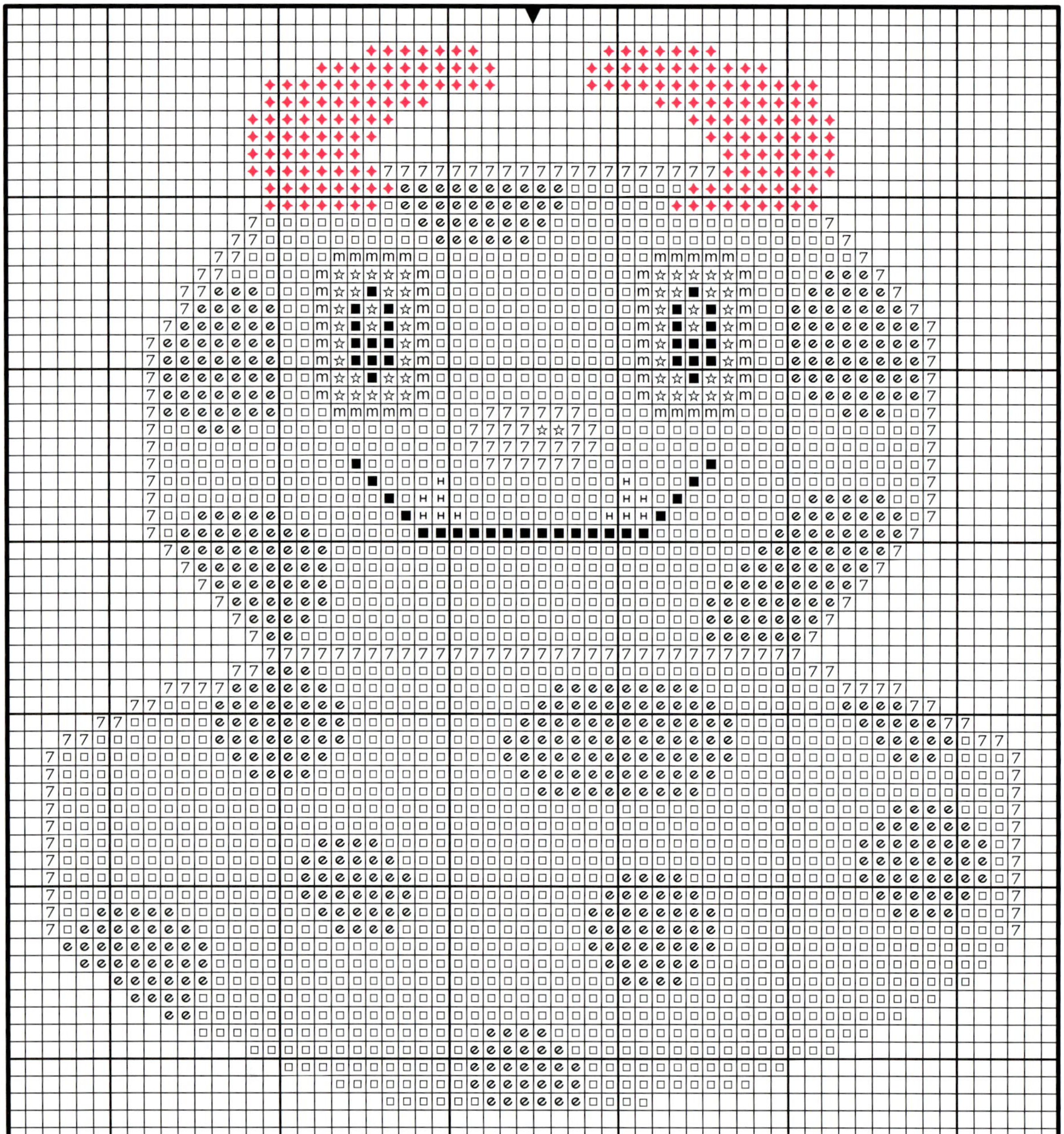

Shown on front cover.

Polka Dotted Monster (58w x 62h)

X	DMC	ANC.	COLOR
☆	blanc	2	white
✦	307	289	yellow
■	310	403	black
H	445	288	lt yellow
e	907	255	green
7	3607	87	plum
□	3609	85	lt plum
m	3844	410	turquoise

Design was stitched on a 14 count Aida white Charles Craft Baby Soft Infant Bib (design size 4¹/₄" x 4¹/₂"), placing the design right above the binding and filling in stitching as necessary. Three strands of floss were used for Cross Stitch.

General Instructions

STITCHING TIP

Working with Floss

To ensure smoother stitches, separate the floss strands and realign them before threading the needle. Keep stitching tension consistent. Begin and end the floss by running under several stitches on the back; never tie knots.

HOW TO READ CHARTS

Each chart is made up of a key and a gridded design on which each square represents a stitch. The symbols in the key tell which floss color to use for each stitch in the chart. The following headings and symbols are given:

X — Cross Stitch
DMC — DMC color number
¼X — Quarter Stitch
B'ST — Backstitch
ANC. — Anchor color number
COLOR — The name given to the floss color in that chart

A square filled with a symbol should be worked as a **Cross Stitch**.

A straight line should be worked as a **Backstitch**.

HOW TO STITCH

Always work **Cross Stitches** first and then add the **Backstitch**. When stitching, bring the threaded needle up at **1** and all **odd** numbers and down at **2** and all **even** numbers.

Cross Stitch (X): For horizontal rows, work stitches in two journeys ***(Fig. 1)***. For vertical rows, complete each stitch as shown ***(Fig. 2)***.

Fig. 1

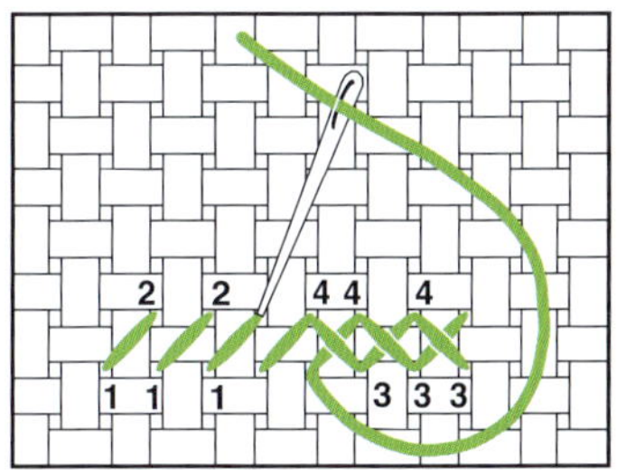

Fig. 2

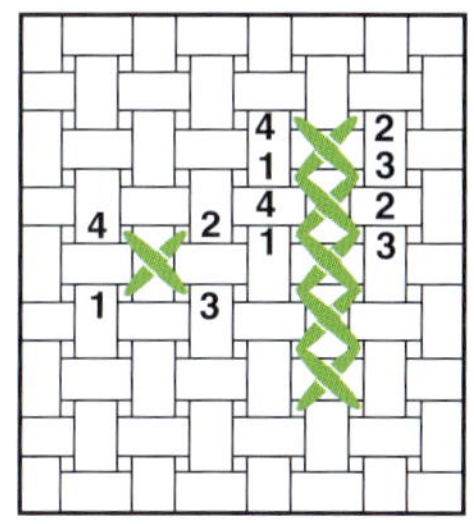

Backstitch (B'ST): For outlines and details, Backstitch should be worked after the design has been completed ***(Fig. 3)***.

Fig. 3

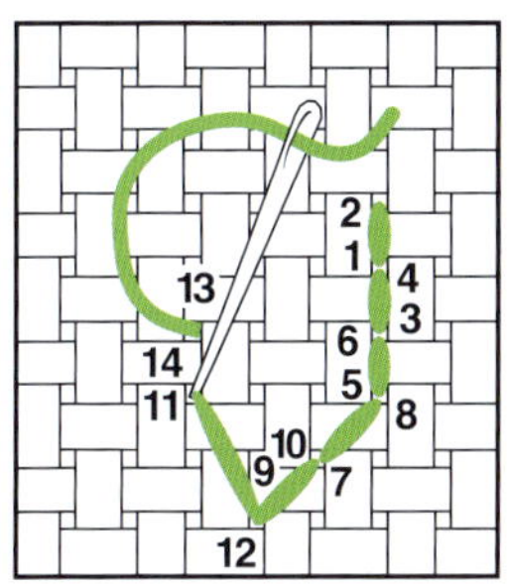

DMC TO SULLIVANS® CONVERSION CHART

This chart lists our suggestions for Sullivans floss substitutions for the DMC floss used in this book.

DMC	SUL	DMC	SUL	DMC	SUL	DMC	SUL
blanc	45001	703	45163	913	45261	3607	45352
157	45472	720	45167	955	45290	3609	45354
164	45479	722	45169	956	45291	3766	45383
208	45040	741	45182	957	45292	3804	45401
209	45041	792	45203	971	45301	3806	45403
307	45051	793	45204	973	45303	3837	45435
310	45053	797	45207	988	45309	3843	45441
444	45099	807	45213	995	45314	3844	45442
445	45100	900	45251	996	45315		
606	45141	906	45255	3347	45344		
666	45155	907	45256	3348	45345		

PRODUCTION TEAM:

Technical Writer – Mary Sullivan Hutcheson; Editorial Writer – Susan McManus Johnson; Senior Graphic Artist – Lora Puls; Graphic Artists - Becca Snider, Angela Ormsby Stark, and Janie Marie Wright; Contributing Photo Stylist - Sondra Daniel; and Contributing Photographer - Ken West.

We have made every effort to ensure that these instructions are accurate and complete. We cannot, however, be responsible for human error, typographical mistakes, or variations in individual work.

Some bibs provided courtesy of Charles Craft, Inc. Embroidery floss provided courtesy of The DMC Corporation.

Instructions tested and photography models made by Gary Hutcheson, Angie Perryman, and Anne Simpson.